THE DECODER

HE SAYS, SHE SAYS

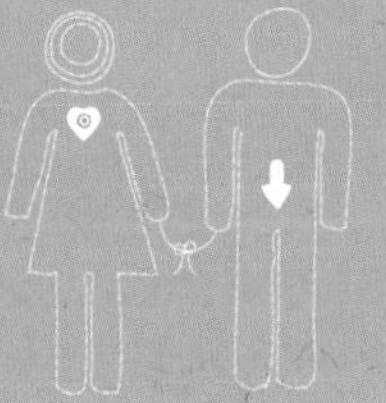

(live, laugh and be happy)

The Decoder: He Says, She Says
by David J. Kuoch

Library of Congress Cataloging-in-Publication Data available.

ISBN: 978-0-9822977-0-4
First edition

Manufactured in China

Book design and layout by Gayheart Design
Copy Editing by Cory Bilicko

Special thanks to Cory, Amy, Morgan, Tanya, Dino, Horace, Adria, Brett, and Katie for the wonderful contributions.

10 9 8 7 6 5 4 3 2

Retired Hipster, Inc.
PO Box 14068
San Francisco, CA 94114

www.retiredhipster.com

$9.95

THE DECODER

HE SAYS, SHE SAYS

MADNESS OF THE MINDS

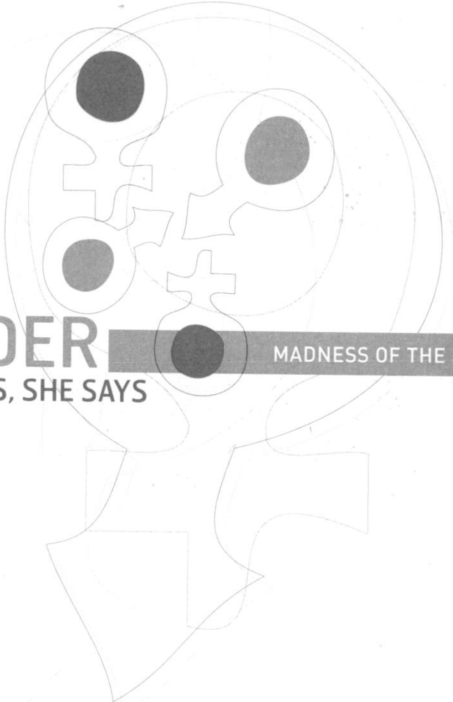

Communications between men and women run the gamut from sheer joy to living hell, depending on our moods and the circumstances we find ourselves in. Often, what we think we heard wasn't actually what was

introduction

intended. Until we've burrowed through the subtexts, alternate agendas, veiled threats, as well as authentic emotions that fill the communication between ourselves and our partners, we tend to sleuth around them in a state of high anxiety until we unearth the **truth.**

The Decoder: He Says, She Says

is a collection of typical clichés that often pass back and forth between the sexes. But what are we really thinking? What are the words that actually come out of our mouths when we really want to say something else? What are the numerous possibilities that exist when we think we're getting a compliment from our significant other? What's the real meaning behind that seemingly innocent question our partner asks?

Why are men often accused of thinking with their "little heads," instead of using logic, while other pathetic saps who try to "read between the lines" discover they were being played by a master manipulator? Why is it that, despite the collections of self-help and relationship books women read, they're often left scratching their heads over some of the things uttered by the men in their lives?

It's no wonder men and women often have communication issues, lying awake at night, replaying verbal scenarios from hours before, wondering who or what to believe. Unfortunately, many men and women simply lack the cajones to ask their partners for the truth.

We understand your pain, fear, and isolation. That not knowing can be confusing, whether it's your first date or after 60 years of matrimony.

Whether you use it for a few good chuckles or as a bedside communication manual, **The Decoder:** He Says, She Says is here to help.

"I DON'T LIKE TO CUDDLE"

...Because then you'll think I care.

I don't like **spooning, nuzzling, hugging, snuggling** or any other girlie activity you consider to be **"romantic".**

What's the point?

Why **cuddle** when you **could be doing more?**

"I don't like to cuddle"

You are ABSOLUTELY NOT my type and I'm still figuring out how the hell I got myself so deep into this situation that you could even THINK ABOUT CUDDLING WITH ME.

. . With anyone
I'm not seriously considering marrying.

KEEP YOUR DISTANCE. You smell funny.

WE'RE NOT HAVING SEX,
SO GET OVER YOURSELF AND TELL ME ANOTHER JOKE.

"You expect too much of me"

You want me to stay awake for this?

Get a job? What, I like living off welfare.

I'm a failure.

Flowers, cards, dinner, messages, compliments, physical attention, saying **"I love you,"** giving you days off from the kids, "talking" whenever you need to, doing the dishes, bringing home the bacon, not saying anything when you justify some trivial expense . . . exactly WHAT am I not doing here?

men women men women men women men women men women men women men women

"You expect too much of me"

No, I'm not wearing high heels to bed! **And put that ridiculous maid costume away.**

WHAT IS THIS, THE ARMY? YOU'RE A CONTROL FREAK.

Maybe your mother liked to do all these things for you, but **she didn't have to sleep with you.**

I just don't think you're the one but I'm going to be the good guy on this one and place all the blame on me.

"I was in a serious relationship before and was hurt so **I'm still trying to get over that"**

Why can't women be more like guys? Have sex when you feel like it and move on!

GOD, SHE WAS A BITCH. YOU'RE NOT LIKE HER, ARE YOU?

How about a pity fuck?

I'm such a good liar, I almost believe me.

"I was in a serious relationship before and was hurt, so I'm still trying to get over that"

I'm still feeling **vulnerable** and will sleep with anyone to **help me forget about him.**

Can't you see I'm licking my wounds right now? JUST HOLD ME AND SHUT UP.

See this baggage? Don't just stand there, help me carry it!

. . . in fact, I wonder who he's with now. God, I miss him. What am I doing here with you?

"I forgot"

It's my lame excuse for telling you that I had no intention of remembering in the first place.

I knew YOU'D REMEMBER.

BAD SIGN. Forgetting an anniversary. I'm gonna have some making up to do.

I had a million things on my mind. Please cut me some slack.

men women men women men women men women men women men women men women

"I forgot"

WHAT? You say it all the time!

I DON'T CARE.

I never forget a thing, SHOULD KNOW THAT!

Oh, let's see. I had to drop off the kids, walk the dog, feed the fish, shop for groceries, mop the floor, vacuum, dust, do laundry, make the beds, prepare the guest room for your mom, write out bills, pick up the kids, chauffeur one to practice, the other to the dentist, come home, make dinner, set the table and have it ready for you with a big old smile on when you arrived.

Yes, I forgot to run your piddle-y little errand. Perhaps, you'd like to trade tomorrow!

"I want someone who is nice"

I'm tired of all the drama. I'm tired of all the maintenance. I'm just tired.
Go fix me a turkey potpie and rub my feet.

No more crazy bitches!

… Nice in public and bad girl in bed.

Someone who will **cook, clean, pick up my laundry, and iron my shirts.**

"I want someone who is nice"

I WANT A MAN WITH A STRONG SENSE OF PERSONAL AUTHORITY AND A FUN, PLAYFUL SIDE, WHO GENUINELY LIKES WOMEN AND DOESN'T ACT LIKE A JERK. MEN TEND TO BE JERKS.
DON'T BE A JERK, OKAY?

The way you yell during football games freaks me out I see violent tendencies.

I want someone that knows I'm right MOST of the time!

I'm looking for someone nice but also adventurous and exciting and great in bed.
Please tell me that's you…Please.

"I'm networking"

Many more fish in the ocean,
if you know what I mean . . .

Have you ever had a **three-way?**

Always looking for an **upgrade . . .**

What? I can't even talk to **another girl?**

"I'M NETWORKING"

I'm setting up shop to see how many awesome dinner dates I can get!

I like the men in your social network,
but I don't like you.

I like to shop for shoes, why not men?

Yes moron, I have a mind for business.

"What attracts me is your mind"

You're not attractive but you're available at the moment.

. . . as for the rest of you . . . well, I'll have to have a couple of drinks first.

. . . your legs, your hips, your eyes . . . just about everything except your mind, actually. I mean no one's actually attracted to a mind. **It's all gray and gooey . . .**

Not exactly a sex-pot, are you?

"WHAT ATTRACTS ME IS YOUR MIND"

You're smart . . . but not as smart as me.

Nope. No chemistry here. Moving on.

You're not my type, but for some reason, I find your intellect so damn sexy.

You're a geek!

"GIVE ME SOME SPACE"

An old girlfriend is in town for the week.

Nag, Nag, Nag,
I can't stand it anymore.

I'm really (claustrophobic) in relationships.

I want to **sleep around** before
getting back together with you.

"GIVE ME SOME SPACE"

Back off, Cling-on!

I'm feeling smothered.

This is not prison and I'm not your bitch.
Back off and let me breathe.

Dude, you were just here this morning. Why are you back?
"I live here." Right, but still…
We need to add an extra wing to the house.

"YOU'RE SO NICE"

FINALLY,
SOMEONE I CAN BRING HOME TO MOM.

....

Buttering you up.

....

You make me FEEL GUILTY.

....

. . . in bed.

"You're so nice"

You can't seriously be this nice.
What are you hiding?

....

THIS "NICE GUY" ACT IS WORKING WELL FOR YOU.
NOW LET'S SEE WHAT YOUR TOLERANCE LEVEL IS.

....

We could never be
anything but friends.

....

You're a complete pushover and
people take advantage of you. GET A LIFE.

"You deserve more"

I was drunk. **That's why I slept with you.**

I'm trying to be considerate of your feelings by letting you know this relationship is going nowhere . . . fast!

It's been real.
Hey, my buddy thinks you're **HOT!**

YOU ARE HIGH MAINTENANCE.

men women men women men women men women men women men women men women

"You deserve more"

YOU WILL **NEVER MEASURE UP** TO MY EXPECTATIONS. **BESIDES, MY OLD BOYFRIEND WANTS ME BACK.**

There are too many ***missing ingredients*** to your recipe. ***It's not working.***

I really like you but the **baggage** is **too hard to overlook.**

I don't really like you *(at least not enough to keep seeing you)* but I can still stroke your ego.

"YES, HONEY"

OUR DEAL:
I SAY YES TO YOU HERE,
YOU SAY YES TO ME LATER.

I heard you the first two times.

At your service.

I hope this "BEING NICE"
routine pays off.

"Yes, honey"

Trying to hide my irritation with you.

AS YOU WISH.

If I sound sweet,
I'll get what I want.

Does it empower your manhood
to hear me say this?

"I love Being Single"

This is just a date. Don't even think about hearing wedding bells 'cause I'm not you're guy.

....

MARRIAGE IS FOR SAPS.

....

I love myself.

....

Hey, I've got a lot of options.
You want to sleep with me?

"I love Being Single"

I hate being single.

I'm only saying this to mask how lonely I am.

....

I'm a black hole of emotional need that, when gurgling to the surface, will eat you alive.

....

I like to keep my options open.
You're cute, BUT NOT THAT CUTE.

....

I hate being single but I don't want to seem needy or desperate.

I don't seem needy or desperate, do I? Do I?

"I was *worried* about you"

Don't you know you're supposed to tell me where you're going **whenever you leave the house?**

Showing concern,
though I don't really care.

ALL DAY I'VE BEEN THINKING ABOUT
HAVING SEX WITH YOU.

Who is he?

"I was *worried* about you"

I DON'T TRUST YOU.

...you selfish bastard.

They should make a **relationship GPS,** then I could just check in at my leisure instead of wondering where **the (bleep) you are!**

Let me guess,
your phone was broken!

"I think I like you!"

I don't have the balls to
tell you how **I really feel.**

Be cool. Let me understate this:
I'm really digging on you and want to see more of you.

You're kind of like an
unattractive buddy, or a sister.

Just gonna play this whole thing down.

"I think I like you!"

I like you, **so don't screw it up.**

I want you to make the first move.
Like... now!

Oh crap, you're smart, funny and actually own property. I'm going to fall for you
and you're going to **hurt me.**

I am starting to feel the **"L" WORD,**
but I don't want to be the first to say it.

"Let's take your car"

Mine's a piece of *crap, trashed, filled with burger wrappers* and *completely out of gas.*

I want to get completely **trashed** tonight so **you should drive.**

MAYBE HAVING **CONTROL** WILL TURN YOU ON.

I forgot to **get gas** and **I'm out of money.**

"Let's take your car"

Open doors, hold my chair and **pick up the check,** and there will be a very special reward for you.

It doesn't have to be **foreign or fast,** just as long as it isn't his parents or stolen.

I want you to drive but I'll be unable to control my backseat driving.

Please, God, tell me has a car.

"It's a guy thing"

There is no rational thought process connected with it, and you have no chance at all of making it.
Logical.

I can't help it. It's the way I'm wired.

I don't want to gross you out.

YOU DON'T WANT TO KNOW THE TRUTH.

"It's a girl thing"

You don't have the capacity to understand that we experience things on an emotional level.

There will be men there, **just not you.**

LOOK, MR. METROSEXUAL. IT'S GIRLS' NIGHT OUT. YES, WE'RE DRINKING AND YES, WE'RE TALKING ABOUT THE STUPID THINGS YOU DO IN BED.

Why do I have to explain everything?

"CAN I HELP WITH DINNER?"

Why isn't dinner already on the table?

....

Who cares about dinner? **Let's have sex.**

....

Please don't say "yes."
I only make Cup O' Noodles.

....

If I pretend to want to help,
will you like me more?

 men women men women men women men women men women men women men women

"CAN I HELP WITH DINNER?"

I might DIE if I eat this.
Move over and let me FIX IT.

....

You look hot.
Can I come watch while you make dinner?

....

LET'S DO THE CUDDLY COUPLE THING
AND MAKE SOMETHING TOGETHER.

....

Look what a pleaser I am.
We're a team!

"I have read all the classics"

I ain't no dumb jock.

I've been subscribing to *Maxim* since 1998.

. . . *The Happy Hooker* . . .
The Joy of Sex . . .

I love Dr. Seuss

"I have read all the classics"

I'M JUST MORE KNOWLEDGEABLE ABOUT LIFE.

Let's find out what Mr. Cro-Magnon knows?

I've read ***some*** of the classics but have definitely seen all the movies.

If he says that *Moby Dick* was his favorite novel, he's a **porn perv** and **I'm outta here.**

"You cook just like my mom"

. . . thank God you don't look like her.

. . . everything is either burnt or has no taste.

Finally, somebody who can cook and clean.

Let's go to McDonalds.

"He's a pig"

I have **secret fantasies** about **this creep.**

He's dirty and stuck up and…
oh, God. I THINK I WANT HIM.

I hate him. **He's a dirtbag.**

He's a narcissistic creep,
but there's something kind of sexy-slimy about him.

"I don't want to ruin our friendship"

I WANT TO SLEEP WITH YOU.
MORE THAN ONCE.
BUT NO COMMITMENT, OKAY?

This is the brush-off!

I am not attracted to you whatsoever, but a little alcohol will help.

I'm willing to
ruin our friendship for sex.

"I don't want to ruin our friendship"

If I have to question if it would ruin our friendship, then I'm not going to do it.

I just don't think we mesh well. It's a chemistry thing.

Dude, you're a creep.
We will never, ever have sex. I repeat: ever.

I'd like to have SEX RIGHT NOW,
then pretend IT NEVER HAPPENED
and *go back to being friends.*

"Honey, we don't need material things to prove our love"

I'm completely broke, so here's a greeting card with flowers on it.

I FORGOT our ANNIVERSARY again.

I'll prove my love to you right now. **Get undressed.**

Why do I have to buy you something to get you to go to bed with me?

"Honey, we don't need material things to prove our love"

I like white gold and diamonds. Emeralds if you're feeling really adventurous.

Let's see if he knows how to craft romance without a gift.

Don't think you can buy me. Show some imagination.

Uh-oh, he knows I'm after the bling.

"It's a really GOOD movie"

It's got explosions, violence, women making out with women, fast cars, and **Jessica Alba.**

. . . for a chick flick.

THE PART WHERE HE CUT OFF HER HEAD WITH A CHAINSAW AND DRANK BLOOD FROM HER NECK WAS AWESOME!

LOTS OF NAKED WOMEN.

men women men women men women men women men women men women men women

"IT'S A REALLY GOOD MOVIE"

I want you to watch the male lead and learn something, moron!

If I have to see one more movie where someone gets decapitated or farts are the main plot points, I may run screaming from the theatre.

Watch this movie and you'll know exactly how I like my romance!

Why can't you be Brad Pitt? **Why?**

"YOU KNOW HOW BAD MY MEMORY IS"

I REMEMBER THE CREDITS OF THE VIDEO GAME, ALL OF ANGELINA JOLIE'S MOVIES, AND ALL THE CARS I'VE EVER OWNED, BUT I FORGOT YOUR BIRTHDAY.

....

I wish I paid more attention when you were telling me the first time.

....

. . . conveniently.

....

For instance, that time **I cheated on you?**
I've even forgotten what her name is.

"YOU KNOW HOW BAD MY MEMORY IS"

I never forget a thing,
you should know that!

....

I didn't forget, I'm trying to catch you in a lie.

....

. . . WHEN IT COMES TO MY MISTAKES.
FOR YOURS, I HAVE A LIST . . .

....

You know how
convenient my memory is. . .

"I will help you clean up around the house"

I once put a dirty towel in the laundry basket.

. . . If you promise me sex whenever I want it.

. . . once every six months.

I'll be responsible for taking out the garbage.

Deal?

"I will help you clean up around the house"

Good thing you're good in bed, because this place is a sty. I need a condom for my whole body. When we're together, you're going to be clean!

Maybe I can fix you. Let's start with your bathroom grout and see where it leads.

. . . and if I do, you owe me one big commitment.

See? I'd be a great wife.

“Have you seen my wallet, keys, watch?”

Act like my mom and help me out here!

....

You’re hiding the damn thing just to spite me!

....

If I can’t find it, it’s not there.

....

I’m too lazy to look for it.

“I’m looking for shoes and a belt to match my skirt.”

I am going to buy out the store by the time I’m finished and tell you how much money I saved by doing so.

....

DEAL WITH IT. I LIKE TO SHOP.

....

I’m high maintenance, but I’m worth it. Now get back to work.

....

Don’t worry, I’m a bargain hunter. I found you, didn’t I?

"WHAT DID I DO THIS TIME?"

Do you just sit around and
WAIT for me to screw things up?

Cut me some slack, your highness!

Did you catch me in a lie?

Good thing I know how to kiss your ass.

"WHAT DID I DO THIS TIME?"

Yes, Mr. Drama?
What terrible thing did I do that I don't care about?

And once again, I failed to be your mother.

I'm not perfect.
I'm sure you'll explain in detail.

OMG, a Stepford husband.

"She's a feminist"

Maybe she'd have a threesome.

....

This is a judgment meant to distance
her from me and you. I don't understand feminism and
I don't want you to either.

....

I admire a woman who stands up for her rights.
Too bad she won't sleep with me.

....

I have a difficult time relating to
women who are not attracted to me.
I find it really unsettling.

"She's a feminist"

She's a BITCH.

....

She's rough around the edges.

....

She's definitely not as hot as I am.
And look at those shoes.

....

You are NOT attracted to HER!

"I hate shopping"

I understand you love to shop, but guys just aren't into it. Unless you're talking cars, power tools and electronics.

I don't care what you look like with clothes on.

I hate standing around with your purse and a cart full of women's clothes while fat ladies eye me amusedly with double strollers filled with screaming kids thinking, "Isn't he cute?"

You're spending too much money.

"I'm not really a big shopper"

With MY money, that is!

Look, I'm not your mother. You're going to have to learn to buy your own clothes…that match.

I don't need to look at fifty different electronic devices. Pick one, get out your card and let's get the hell outta here!

WE CAN'T AFFORD ANYMORE OF YOUR "TOYS."

"I'M GOING OUT WITH THE GUYS"

I want to escape from you and drink myself into a shit-faced stupor.

Life sucks. And you're the cause.

I'M GOING TO GO GET DRUNK AND FLIRT WITH THE WAITRESSES AT HOOTERS.

You're driving me to drink.

"I'M GOING OUT WITH THE GIRLS"

I'm spending money and I don't want to hear about it!

WE'RE GOING OUT TO TALK ABOUT MEN, RELATIONSHIPS, AND YOUR INABILITY TO PLEASE ME.

This is my time to have fun. Maybe you should go out with your boys.

I need to talk about you so I can be with you!

"I heard you"

I haven't the faintest clue what you just said, and I'm hoping desperately that I can fake it well enough so that you don't spend the next 3 days yelling at me.

....

I have no idea what you said,
but you can stop talking now.

....

Once is enough. **Quit nagging me.**

....

I have every intention to be sensitive to your needs…
right after the game.

"Why do you wash the dishes, clean the floor, fold clothes like that?"

You are doing it all wrong.
Why can't you do it my way?

....

Playing stupid does not excuse you from household chores. But nice try!

....

I'm going to make a suggestion on how you could do it differently.

....

You have **no domestic skills.**
Good thing **you're hot in bed.**

"No, pizza's fine"

Anything is better than your cooking.

If I have to eat another vegan tofu salad,
I will slit my wrist.

YOUR ASS IS GOING TO
GET BIGGER THOUGH.

. . . everyday. Pizza is fine everyday.

"No, pizza's fine"

If he uses the coupons, IT'S OVER.

I guess the magic has worn off. FYI . . . If we're having slices, we're definitely not having sex.

Pizza and beer are for college,
NOT FIRST DATES.

This place is interesting:
I guess McDonald's was booked up.

"LET'S TALK"

Fine. Let's get this over with. Two hours of you whining about your "feelings." It's okay. Get it out of your system. I'm here for you, you big baby.

. . . ABOUT SEX.

I am trying to impress you by showing you that I'm sensitive and understanding.

I've spent months and months rehearsing this moment and these are the only words I can think of to say, **"Adios."**

men women men women men women men women men women men women men women

"Let's talk"

THINGS NEED TO CHANGE MY WAY.
YEP, MY WAY OR THE HIGHWAY.

I'm going to talk and you're going to shut your mouth and listen.

If you ever do that again, **IT'S OVER!**

I'm trying to be patient and understanding, **but you're a moron.**

"You look terrific"

Oh, God, please don't try on one more outfit.
I can't sit through another ensemble change.

I'll say anything to make you happy.
God knows, life's a bitch when you're not.

WHAT THE HELL ELSE AM I GOING TO SAY? OF COURSE I LIKE IT, HONEY.

You always look terrific. You turn me on no matter what you're wearing.

"You look terrific"

Oh, no. Not even *Queer Eye for the Straight Guy* can help you.

He can't be serious about that shirt with those pants. Oh wait, he is serious.

PLEASE, don't let anyone we know see us!

I've got to pick my battles,
but as soon as this gets serious,
I'm finding you an image consultant.

"I brought you a present"

My ex-girlfriend left this in my closet.

THE OFFICE WAS GIVING AWAY FREE T-SHIRTS.

. . . Right here in my shorts, baby.

I want to give you everything you ever want . . . and more. YOU DESERVE IT.

"I brought you a present"

This is what people do to show they love each other. Pay attention and take notes.

I'm moving in. **My stuff is in the car.**

How you treat this gift will tell me how important I am to you.

. . . WHAT DID YOU GET ME?

"I DON'T NEED TO READ THE INSTRUCTIONS"

I am perfectly capable of screwing
it up without your help.

. . . If I'm wrong, THEN I'LL READ THEM.

. . . I've got you right here telling me what to do.

Eventually, I'll figure it out.
No matter how many times I mess it up.

"We're moving too quickly"

Love? I don't even know if I like you.

Back off.

I see a lifetime of control freaking.
Need to back up and re-group.

Hold up there, Sparky. Time to end it.

"I'll take you to a nice restaurant"

I'm spending money on this meal,
so you better have sex with me.

....

It doesn't have a drive-thru.

....

I'm completely broke, so maybe next time.

....

. . . How much are the burgers at Denny's?

"You're so manly"

YOU NEED TO SHAVE AND SHOWER,
AND STOP SWEATING LIKE A PIG.

....

Thank God we don't have to hire someone
to do all this. You're wonderful, honey!

....

. . . down there.

....

How about a shower, this millennium!

"I RECYCLE"

We could pay the rent with the money
from my empty beer cans.

Really, I walk around parks with a shopping cart. . .

. . . my girlfriends.

I'm environmentally conscious, AND SENSITIVE.
Doesn't that turn you on?

"This kitchen is so small"

MAKE SOME MONEY SO WE
CAN UPGRADE.

I want a new home.

This place is a dump and I'm going to start
throwing a fit on a daily basis.

TIME TO MOVE OR REMODEL.

"I broke up with her"

SHE DUMPED ME.

I'm still **in love with her** and it's going to take some **time to get over her.**
But I'd like to keep seeing you, if that's okay.

I am not *sleeping with her* at the moment.

She won't return my calls.

"I broke up with him"

I caught him cheating on me.

DON'T WORRY, IT'S OVER.
(FINGERS CROSSED)

I went a little crazy when we broke up.
But I'm all better now and usually don't throw things.

Wow, he still looks really good, doesn't he?

"You look stressed, let me give you a massage"

Take off your shirt, please.

....

You realize if you accept this massage, I'm going to want something in return . . . nudge, nudge.

....

I'd like to touch your breasts,
let me give you a massage.

....

Closer . . . closer . . .
Almost have you in my clutches.

"Do I look fat?"

If you ever want to have sex again, you'll tell me what I need to hear.

....

You better tell me that the reason
your eyes drifted to my ass
is because you want to touch it!

....

I feel fat. Am I? Lie to me.
Tell me how cute I am . . . **I really need it.**

....

You know the answer to this one. It's "no." And that's a no, with no frills or add-ons like "you look happy" or "you look plump" or you look "rested." Just a plain old "no," that's it.

"Are you seeing anyone right now?"

I really like you and want to go out with you but I'm nervous, so I'll just ask you . . .

. . . If you're on the market, I'm buying.

ARE YOU SLEEPING WITH ANYONE RIGHT NOW?

. . . if you are, would you dump him for me?

"Are you seeing anyone right now?"

Only one answer that I want to hear and it starts with **"N"** and ends in **"O"**.

WHY ARE YOU SINGLE? WHAT'S WRONG WITH YOU? PSYCHO? GAY?

Hint: When are you going to ask me out?

You better not be dating anyone right now. You are now on the short list for boyfriend.

"Do you really want to go to that restaurant, movie, dinner party?"

I don't want to go.

....

I'm too cheap
to spend any money on you.

....

There won't be any hot chicks there.

....

I'm too tired to get gussied up and pretend that I like those people.

"Do you really want to go to that restaurant, movie, dinner party?"

I know you don't want to go but I want you to want to or at least pretend to want to because you know how happy it will make me and you love making me happy.

....

You'll ignore me all night long.

....

IF I'M GOING TO HAVE TO BABYSIT YOUR NEEDS TONIGHT, I'D RATHER YOU STAY HOME AND I'LL GO ALONE.

....

You didn't seem very excited, I want to make sure you're not going just because I want to go.

"YOU'RE GREAT WITH KIDS"

Uh-oh! What have I done! I just used one of the most potent pick-up lines off all time.

Too bad we'll never have any together. I've had a vasectomy.

...That's good because I need a babysitter.

I CAN TELL BY HOW YOU TREAT ME WHEN I'M ACTING CHILDISH.

"You're great with kids"

Surprise! I'm pregnant!

I need to find out if you're into kids without sounding like a psycho on a time clock.

I'm thinking one boy and one girl. Maybe twins. But we can start slow. How about a puppy?

Maybe we can make babies together.

"Are you close to your family?"

I hope you're not too close.
I don't want to have to hold myself accountable to anyone Else.

....

This will tell me a lot about you . . .

....

If your family is anything like you, I really need to think twice about this relationship.

....

Any history of incest or abuse?

"Are you close to your family?"

Okay, what's wrong with YOUR family?

....

The right answer is YES but not too close.
You see them on holidays and summer vacations.
And you definitely don't live in their basement.

....

Will I have to attend every family reunion and every holiday function?

....

Do you come from a lineage of psychos, because I think mental illness is hereditary, which means our kids will be nightmares.

"I COULD NEVER LIE TO YOU"

Don't ask me about things you don't want to know about.

. . . unless I had to.

YOU'RE TOO GOOD AT SNIFFING OUT THE B.S.

I'm lying now because . . . **I can and I have.**

"I could never lie to you"

And by lie, you mean . . . ?

As long as you buy this,
I can ALWAYS lie to you.

And by lie, I mean big lies. There will probably always be small white lies. Like I love your impressions, and your mother's cooking is the best in the world.

NEVER REAL LIES . . . MAYBE A FEW WHITE ONES THAT MAKE EVERYTHING RUN SMOOTHLY...?

"I promise, I'll change"

I've never changed before
but this time **I mean it.**

I'm hoping you believe me.
I'm beginning to doubt it myself.

What do I need to say to keep you . . . ?

How the hell am I going to change *that?*

"I promise, I'll change"

I'M WILLING TO **CHANGE** IF YOU ARE.

No chance in hell I'll change.

You shouldn't want me to change. You should adore me just like I am. But sure, I promise.

I really blew it. I'd better promise to change.

"You do what you want"

. . . and I'll do what I want.

Go ahead. Stubborn bitch. See if I care.

Turnabout is fair play.

You don't need **my permission.**

"You do what you want"

Payback is a **bitch.**

I am going to **make your life miserable** if you don't **guess what I really want you to do.**

You do what you want and we're over.

You do what I want and things will be just fine.

Yes, I do like **"20 Questions"** and I want you to ask me what I would rather do. I thought we were a team!

"There's no one else"

...unless somebody better comes along.

Stop being paranoid.

How did you know?

. . . yet.

"There's no one else"

...that you know of.

Okay, I did sleep with my ex-boyfriend last week, but that doesn't really count.

THERE WAS. BUT NOT NOW.
SO, I'M NOT LYING. NO ONE ELSE.

. . . Well, there is . . . but I'm dumping him for you after tonight.

"Oh, yes. Right there"

Don't move.

CAN WE DO THIS AGAIN AS SOON AS WE'RE DONE?

I'll take this woman to be my lawfully wedded wife . . .

Don't stop doing that.

"Oh, yes. Right there"

I said "right there" for a reason because you've gone everywhere but there. Now don't lose your way again...wait!

Do that. Again and again and . . . again.

Life partner! Right there. You just sealed the deal. If you're willing to do THAT every night, SIGN. ME. UP!

How long can you hold that position?

"It didn't mean anything, I SWEAR"

This is **my lame attempt** at trying to justify **why I cheated on you.**

I was thinking with the little head.

Not the big one.

I don't even remember it,
I was so wasted.

Seriously, it meant about as much as pizza and beer.

"It didn't mean anything, I SWEAR"

I need more sex and romance. Hear me?
I need some romance!

I swear I'll eventually forget what it meant to me.

I THOUGHT IT WOULD BE FUN AND NOW
I FEEL LIKE A CHEAP-ASS WHORE.
CAN YOU FORGIVE ME?

Pay more attention to me or I'll do it again,
I swear.

"I'LL CALL YOU"

Does a late-night booty call
in a drunken stupor count?

I could definitely see us bumping uglies.

. . . and call you. And I'll keep calling.
Cause I re-e-e-ally like you.
And I think we could be great friends. Eeee heee . . .

I will never call you.

I don't even have your number. I'm just saying this because this is what you say at the end of a date when you have absolutely no intention of ever seeing that person again in your life.

"I'll call you"

Standard closing remarks.

It doesn't mean anything.

I'M JUST TAKING YOUR NUMBER FOR THE SAKE OF BEING NICE. I DON'T PLAN ON CALLING YOU EVER, OR MIGHT CALL YOU WHEN

I NEED A FAVOR.

I will call you so I don't have to wait for you to call me.

I'm tired of that game!

. . . Right. I'd have to be pretty damn desperate.

"YOU LOOK UPSET"

I guess sex is out of the question.

....

...I just pissed you off, **right?**

....

Sorry about what I said previously.
Um, what did I say again?

....

BUSTED!

"You look upset"

What did I do now?

....

Let me in! I want to know every last thing about you, figure this relationship out, and start planning our wedding.
Hello? Knock-knock.

....

Haven't I pleased you master, haven't I?

....

YOU LOOK PSYCHOTIC!

"I love you"

Let's have sex.

I can't stop thinking about you. I'm obsessed.

I need to ask you for a **big favor.**

I'M YOURS.

men women men women men women men women men women men women men women

I need you to tell me that you love me.

You make me feel whole.
Now, marry me.

I LOVE THE WAY OUR FANTASY LIFE
LOOKS IN MY HEAD.

I want to get married, have children,
and live the rest of my life in bliss.

"I love you"

"We're going to be late"

Now I have a legitimate excuse to drive like a maniac.

What takes you **so long to get ready?**

It's **not my fault** that we're late.

I'm sorry I waited until the last minute to get ready.

"We're going to be late"

Hurry your ass up!

You have no concept of time and I'm so done nagging at you.

I'm not ready and it's up to you to make the call and tell them **"we"** are running late.

You're ruining my life!

"Let's meet at the bar. I'll be there with friends"

I want to have a few drinks before you get there so you don't know how drunk I am.

....

MY FRIENDS ARE BRINGING THEIR GIRLFRIENDS AND A COUPLE OF THEM ARE PRETTY HOT. **I WANT A CHANCE TO HIT ON THEM BEFORE YOU GET THERE.**

....

You're my backup plan
in case something better doesn't come along.

....

. . . THIS WAY IF I LEAVE WITH SOMEONE ELSE BEFORE YOU GET THERE,
I CAN ALWAYS BLAME THE GUYS.

men **women** *men* **women** *men* **women** *men* **women** *men* **women** *men* **women** *men* **women**

"Let's meet at the bar. I'll be there with friends"

I DO like the dangerous types but I'm not sure I want to be alone with you.

....

I LIKE YOU, BUT I NEED
A SECOND OPINION.

....

I don't want to give you the wrong idea:
this is by no means a date.

....

It's time for the red-light,
green-light from my friends. **Good luck!**

"I'll never tell"

Let's do it and keep it a secret.

I understand how embarrassing it would be for this to be made public. Your secret's safe with me.

. . . ALL THAT HAPPENED.

If I promise not to tell, what will you do for me?

"I'll never tell"

I'll never be able to keep **THIS SECRET.**

EMBARRASSING...
YOU BETTER HOPE I DON'T TELL.

You're off limits, so if you don't tell,
I won't.

Feel free to share everything:
I'M TELLING EVERYONE.

“Give me a call sometime”

I am not interested enough to chase you, but sex would be okay.

I’LL WAIT BY THE PHONE TO *69 YOU.

You want me . . . you know you do.

If you’re ever hungry and want to grab a bite to eat . . . if you’re lonely, tired, upset, need someone to talk to, horny, (especially horny), or want to have a good time. . . .

“Give me a call sometime”

I am not interested enough to chase you, but you can chase me if you want to.

Erase my number or pretend I don’t exist.

Promise you’ll call me, okay? PROMISE!

I’M REALLY TRYING TO BE CASUAL AND ACT LIKE I DON’T CARE IF YOU CALL ME OR NOT....BUT, PLEEEEEEASE CALL.

"She's just a friend"

She used to be "just a friend" until we slept together. Now she's "just somebody I'd like to sleep with again."

. . . She is. I wish she was something more but, alas, I'm not that lucky.

You need to stop being so suspicious of me.

. . . WITH BENEFITS.

"He's just a friend"

. . . when you're around.

DON'T GO STALKER ON ME.

Jealous? Good!

He's an idiot, but he makes me laugh.
Do not emulate him if you want to keep sleeping with me.

"I want to stay home with you tonight"

My tivo is on the fritz, can I watch the game tonight?

I'M BROKE, SO LET'S STAY IN.

I want us to do it as many times as we can tonight. Let's set a record.

I've been walking around with a hard-on all day and was hoping to do something about it.

"I WANT TO STAY HOME WITH YOU TONIGHT"

I am PMS-ing, feeling fat and bloated and want to be left alone.

If you play your cards right, you'll get a special treat.

Let's cuddle, watch a movie, and eat double-stuffs on the couch.

YOU'RE UP TO SOMETHING. I THINK I'LL STAY HOME AND FOIL YOUR PLANS!

“What time do you need to go to work?”

Do we have time for a quickie?

....

You are **annoying me** and

I can’t wait for you to leave.

....

AS SOON AS YOU LEAVE,
I’M GOING TO MASTURBATE.

....

I’m hoping you’ll get out
of here so I can get some work done.

“What time do you need to go to work?”

I’ve got a list of things I’d like you
to do before you go.

....

WHAT TIME DO
I FINALLY GET RID OF YOU?

....

I want sex. Do we have time to
fit this into the schedule?

....

Still here? GET OUT before I lose it!

"Let's be romantic and turn out the lights"

Eww! Stretch marks.

I have a blemish on my penis, but it's fine! I just don't want you to freak.

I want to score so bad. I need to make sure I say all the right things . . .

YOU WERE BETTER LOOKING IN THE BAR.

"Let's be romantic and turn out the lights"

This body is a war zone of scars and stretch marks, but in the dark, we're all good.

I don't like to feel like I'm in an exam room during sex, so turn off the lights or I'm outta here.

There's something I need to tell you. . .

Don't need to see your penis, thanks!

"You are mysterious"

What are you hiding from me?

You are probably more of a **"whore"** than me.

I'M HAVING A HARD TIME READING WHAT **YOU'RE THINKING AND FEELING.** I CAN'T FIGURE YOU OUT.

With you, there's more than meets the eye.

"You are mysterious"

Weirdo.

TELL ME WHAT YOU'RE THINKING OR I'LL START MAKING SHIT UP.

Enough with the moody-man syndrome. What the heck is your problem?

I don't trust you.

"It was just sex. It didn't mean anything"

Dinner, drinks, dancing . . .
I invested a lot in getting laid. YOU'RE RIGHT.
It was more than just sex. I EARNED IT!

. . . .

I'm sorry, I was drunk . . . and really really horny.

Not a good combination for fidelity.

. . . .

If we had sex more often
this wouldn't happen.

. . . .

What am I saying?
Of course it meant something. IT WAS SEX!

"It was just sex. It didn't mean anything"

IT WAS JUST SEX.
PRETTY DAMN GOOD SEX!

. . . .

Oh, how I wish this were true.
It'd make life a lot easier.

. . . .

Let me persuade you into believing
that I had no emotional or
physical investment in this whatsoever.

. . . .

SEE? THAT'LL SHOW YOU.
PAY ATTENTION TO ME OR I'LL SCREW AROUND.

"I lived with a woman once, but it didn't work out"

Been there, done that . . .
and I doubt that it will work out this time.

I'm not ready to
hand over my cajones.

I'm giving you a disclaimer:
I'm not a suitable person to live with.

Not interested in the
clutter of all your clothes.

"I lived with a man once, but it didn't work out"

I caught him cheating on me
and threw him out.

He was a complete slob.

He wouldn't do anything I said!

DON'T EVEN THINK ABOUT ASKING ME
TO MOVE IN...UNLESS WE'RE MARRIED.

"We'll just cuddle for a minute"

I'LL JUST PUT MY HANDS ON YOUR BREASTS.

Let me get a quick nap in, and then
I'm good to go again.

This is a lame excuse for trying to cop a feel.

Oh, have I tired you out? We'll just cuddle for a minute. **Then it's right back at it.**

"WE'LL JUST CUDDLE FOR A MINUTE"

Uh, wrong time of the month.
This is awkward.

I'M HORNY AS HELL,
but I don't want you to know it.

I'M TOO TIRED FOR SEX.
MAYBE WE'LL BOTH FALL ASLEEP.

WRONG! That's all we'll be doing tonight.

“Tell me about your ex-boyfriend”

Tell me about the losers and creeps you dated.

Who has the BIGGER PENIS?

Why did he dump you?
I want to know what I’m getting myself into here.

Am I a better lover?

“Tell me about your ex-girlfriend”

Tell me what not to be/do.

TELL ME SHE WASN’T THAT
PRETTY/ THIN/ SMART.

Tell me about the
SLUTS AND WHORES
you dated.

Are you trying to repeat the same mistake again?
I understand bad habits are hard to break.

"I still find you attractive"

It doesn't matter how old you are. You're still hot.

The scars are **hardly noticeable.**

I'll sleep with you, if he won't.

...when you're wearing makeup.

"I still find you attractive"

No matter what anyone says. . .

Stop talking. **Let's have sex.**

No need to hold a grudge. **Let's have make-up sex.**

WE ARE OBVIOUSLY SEXUALLY ATTRACTED . . . BUT IT DOESN'T MEAN THAT I WANT TO BE INVOLVED WITH YOU.

"I haven't seen her since we broke up"

SHE GOT A RESTRAINING ORDER.

I'm afraid of what might happen if I DID see her. I still have feelings for her.

. . . I've called her, but haven't seen her.

She vowed never to speak to me again.

"I haven't seen him since we broke up"

...but we still talk on the phone

Not counting the late-night drive-bys.

BUT IF I DID SEE HIM I'D KICK THAT ROTTEN S.O.B. SQUARE IN THE BALLS!

But I think about him every day.

You don't know where he is, do you?

"I really love our time together"

I only want to see you part-time and **I'm incapable of making this a full-time commitment.**

How the hell are you

driving me this crazy so soon?

We're friends who get each other off without having to deal with the **emotional baggage** a **deeper relationship entails.**

. . . but I'm not ready for a relationship.

"I really love our time together"

I'm head over heals

crazy in love with you. Are you?

You will only be a friend and nothing more will come from this relationship.

I want to see you more often. **I'm obsessed!**

I'M REALLY FALLING FOR YOU.

NOTICE HOW I USED "LOVE" IN A SENTENCE?

"I meant to call you this weekend"

IT'S TOO MUCH EFFORT TO GET YOU INTO BED, SO I DECIDED TO JUST STAY HOME AND PERUSE PORN SITES.

Didn't you say you were going to call me this weekend?

I got wasted with my buddies and was way too hung-over to call.

Why am I justifying my actions to you?

"I MEANT TO CALL YOU THIS WEEKEND"

I'm taken right now so don't waste your time.

I'M AVOIDING YOU. Don't ever call me back. Even better, lose my number.

I'M STALKING YOU AND DON'T WANT YOU TO KNOW ABOUT IT.

I'm out of your league. FORGET IT, FRODO!

“WE SHOULD SEE OTHER PEOPLE”

I need to sow a few more wild oats before settling down.

I'm not a ONE-WOMAN GUY.

I'm trying to ease my way out of this relationship.

Once I have something, I always wonder what's next.

“We should see other people”

ALL OF A SUDDEN GUYS ARE SHOWING UP OUT OF THE WOODWORK. JUST CHECKING MY OPTIONS.

I'm having **second thoughts… and third ones.**

I must leave my options open because you're not that interesting and if you're all I get…well, I guess we might be able to make it work.

This is what happens when you get too cocky. You need to work for it, buddy.

"WHERE IS THIS RELATIONSHIP GOING?"

Put that dildo away!

....

Please don't try to force
a commitment out of me.

....

YOU ARE A NUT JOB.
JUST WHAT EXACTLY DO YOU EXPECT FROM ME?

....

What SPELL have you put on me?

"Where is this relationship going?"

I know what I want. *What do you want?*
I can't figure you out.

....

I WANT TO KNOW IF THERE
IS A FUTURE FOR US. OTHERWISE I NEED TO
RE-EVALUATE MY OPTIONS.

....

Why is the BLOW-UP DOLL
coming to bed with us?

....

If we don't get *married* soon
I will leave you.

"It's not you, it's me"

IT'S YOU! Believe me, it's you. I'm just glad to be getting out of this mess once and for all.

I'll make this easy. I'LL TAKE THE BLAME.

Poor thing. This is going to crush her.
Maybe I can soften the blow. . .

Of course it's you, you live in a fairyland,
you over-entitled daddy's girl.

IT IS YOU. SORRY. I'VE GOT A PICTURE *(in my head)*
. . . AND YOU LOOK NOTHING LIKE IT.

I'm ***never*** happy ***with what*** I have.

Whether it's you or me, or everyone we know,
IT'S NOT GOING TO WORK.

You bring out the worst in me.
So actually, it's you.

"It's not you, it's me"

"LET'S BE FRIENDS"

While I'd be **happy to have sex** with you right now, I'd lose interest in you over the long haul.

I want to remain friends... **with benefits.**

SEX WITHOUT STRINGS, *whattaya say?*

Having sex with you **regularly** is much more **appealing** to me than getting **caught up** in all the **trappings of a relationship.**

"Let's be friends"

I'm not interested in you but I am very interested in one of your friends. **Could you set us up?**

While I appreciate the offer, **I don't think sleeping together is such a good idea.**

I'M SORRY.
THE LAST TIME WE HAD SEX WAS VERY DISAPPOINTING.

Don't hold your breath for this **to ever become sexual.**

"I NEED A BIG FAVOR..."

If you want out of this relationship, now would be a good time to go. Once the mooching starts, it doesn't stop.

....

I can't afford my rent. **Can I move in?**

....

It sucks that I have to do this. . .

....

Warning: **I'm a bum.** I'm a selfish, self-centered louse who has no qualms with using people. I'm going to suck you bone-dry and afterwards you will thank me for my kindness. Essentially, at the core, **I'm a terrible person.** If you fail to heed this warning your life will be ruined. **Run.** While there's still time. **Run for your life.**

"I need a big favor..."

Please put on this **Superman outfit** and rescue me.

....

I KNOW YOU DON'T WANT ME TO ASK, BUT I'LL ASK ANYWAYS.

....

Get out your wallet.

....

I'm going to use you and you'll actually be glad that I did because of the nice way I do it.

"I need some time to figure things out"

I'm trying to figure out an easy way to let you down.

I don't CARE anymore.

. . . Like how I'm going to DUMP YOU.

I'm not quite ready to let you go but want to DATE OTHER GIRLS.

"I need some time to figure things out"

I want us to take a BREAK.

Letting you down the easy way.

I'm completely fed up with you. GET LOST.

I'M NOT QUITE READY TO LET YOU GO BUT IT DOESN'T MEAN YOU CAN SLEEP AROUND.

"I'M TIRED"

I want to watch the game.

NO, I'm not getting up to do that.

I CAN'T LISTEN TO YOU NOW.

Can't you see how hard I'm working?

"I'm tired"

You're annoying me.

I'm really not in the mood.
You want to get off? It's shaking hands with Mr.Happy or nothing for you.

I'm on my period.

WE'RE NOT HAVING SEX TONIGHT.
My brain can't wrap around the thought and my legs can't wrap around you. GOOD NIGHT.

"What will people be wearing?"

Can I wear what I'm wearing now?

What kind of PEOPLE will be at this party?

Will there be any HOT CHICKS?

Are these people **stuck up** or **down to earth?**

"What will people be wearing?"

Who do you want as your date tonight?
The whore, the girl-next-door or the librarian?

I WANT TO LOOK SEXY, BUT NOT SLUTTY.
BUT SLUTTY-SEXY MIGHT BE OKAY,
DEPENDING ON WHAT THE OTHER GIRLS ARE WEARING.

You never think about these things.
HELP ME OUT HERE.
I don't want to show up looking like a complete ass.

I don't want to BE UNDER-DRESSED,
appear like I spent too much time, or too little time,
but also not be over-dressed, YET STYLISH, BUT ORIGINAL.

"I DON'T KNOW"

You're the know-it-all. **You tell me.**

There's nothing
I can say that will satisfy you.

If I play stupid, maybe she'll let it go.

I don't have a
LIE HANDY FOR THIS SITUATION.

men women men women men women men women men women men women men women

"I DON'T KNOW"

I know everything.

I know but some things are better kept private

I DON'T KNOW WHERE YOUR
WALLET, KEYS OR PHONE ARE. EVEN IF I DO,
I'M NOT TELLING YOU. GET A PURSE.

Of course I know, you know I know,
but you never listen to me, so, take this . . .

"Let's have some fun and see where this ends up"

I'M READY FOR A NIGHT OF DEBAUCHERY.

DRINK UP, DRINK UP.
It'll be easier to get you to go to bed with me if you're drunk.

I'm so horny right now all I can think about is getting into your pants.

Why are you stopping?
We were just starting to have fun.

"Let's have some fun and see where this ends up"

I'm playful.
Remember this when I get serious.

I'M 99% SURE YOU'RE "THE ONE." BUT I DON'T WANT TO SCARE THE SHIT OUT OF YOU, SO WE'RE GOING TO KEEP IT LIGHT...FOR AT LEAST TWO WEEKS.

. . . with the emphasis on
"where this ends up." Say, in wedding vows?

I'm tricking you into believing I actually want a carefree, casual, uncommitted relationship, just so you want me more. **Working, isn't it?**

"Are you listening to me?"

Is this too complicated for you?

Do I have to **repeat everything** I just said?

Heal. Stay . . . Good girl.

Wake up and pay attention.

men women men women men women men women men women men women men women

"Are you listening to me?"

Do you have ADD?

THIS IS NOT TIVO; YOU CAN'T PLAY ME BACK LATER.

If I have to ask you, then you already know that you have not been listening to me.

These lips have words coming out of them, stop fantasizing and listen.

"I'm not yelling!"

I'm not yelling!
THIS! THIS IS YELLING!

I'm not yelling! I'm talking with emphasis.

Stop trying to control everything!
I'm yelling because I'm trying to be heard.
Now, shut up and listen!

What, I'm now allowed a little human emotion?
Give me a minute to cool down.

"I'm not yelling!"

Yes, I'm yelling because this is important.

I'm not yelling!
My voice always sounds this way in response to overbearing control freaks.

Of course I'm yelling! **I'm really good at it!**

This is passion! *Deal with it!*

"We need to talk"

Things need to change or I'm out of here.

Um...I have this little sore,
but I don't think it's contagious.

I've got some bad news.

Young lady, you are in trou...BLE!

men women men women men women men women men women men women men women

"We need to talk"

You are in big trouble, mister.

WE HAVE A PROBLEM.
I'M NOT HAPPY!

You need to listen.

I want to complain.

“I'll be ready in a minute”

You better hurry up,
I'm leaving in exactly 60 seconds.

I know the wedding is about to start . . .

. . . I need to pinch a loaf.

Get ready.

“I'll be ready in a minute”

I'm TRYING to find something
I look good in.

I'll be ready when I'm ready...
definitely taking longer than I know I should be taking.

I am ready, but I'm going to make you wait
because I know you have to.

Take your pick, 5, 10, 15, 30, 45 minutes,
or when I'm good and ready.

"I like your friends, but . . ."

What do you tell your friends about me?

I've never liked any of your friends; they're judgmental and hostile toward me.

What a bunch of bitches!

None of your friends will sleep with me.

"I like your friends, but . . ."

Your friends are losers.

I don't like the way you behave when you are around them.

You were much sexier before I met your friends.

. . . DO YOU HAVE TO KEEP THEM?

"I like that girl's hair"

What would you think of a threesome with that girl?

You're cute, but your hair sucks. This is what I like . . .

I wish I was with her, not you.

I'm sensitive enough to notice things like hair and clothes, tits and ass . . .

"I like that guy's hair"

I'm going to cheat on you with Sexy Hair Guy if you don't do something about your mullet, sideburns, comb-over, dandruff.

YOUR HAIR LOOKS RIDICULOUS.

Take a hint, I'm trying to make you jealous.

Maybe we could do something different with yours.

"I'm leaving, but feel free to stay if you like"

TAKE A HINT.

Get out.

I'd rather be here than to go with you.

I don't want you **snooping around** my place while I'm gone.

"I'm leaving, but feel free to stay if you like"

Please don't be here when I get back.

THERE'S NO WAY I'M LEAVING UNTIL YOU LEAVE.

Why are you still here?

You better come with me if you know what's good for you.

"I miss you"

I'm **completely lost** when you're not around...
I can't find my shoes, the kids are starved,
and **we're out of beer.**

I can't tell you the L.O.V.E. word,
so it's my way of expressing myself.

. . . having sex with you.

There's no one here to cook for me, or do the dishes,
the laundry, the shopping. No one to vacuum, to walk the dog,
TO HAVE SEX WITH ME! *Please come home.*

"I miss you"

You're not the jerk I thought you were.

I'M LONELY,
OKAY, HORNY TOO.

...the way you used
to pay for everything.

I don't have anyone to yell at.

"I know where I'm going"

SHUT UP AND LET ME DRIVE!
BACK-SEAT BITCH!

I'm completely lost and
I'm too proud to stop and ask for directions.

. . . I'm going crazy because of your back-seat driving, self-righteous remarks, and know-it-all attitude.

. . . We are so lost.
Screw it, let's just make the best of it.

"Why don't you try to kiss me like this?"

Ease up on the saliva,
I already took a shower today.

IT'S OKAY,
I'LL TEACH YOU HOW I LIKE IT.

Did I rescue a Saint Bernard?
I'm being assaulted by saliva.

How experimental are you?

"I THINK OF YOU AS A SISTER"

ALL WE DO IS SQUABBLE.

I really respect you and don't think you deserve the crap I'm about to pull.

. . . and it'd be weird to sleep with your **sister.**

Want to keep you close to me, but not that close.

 men women men women men women men women men women men women men women

"I think of you as a brother"

There is absolutely no way we are having sex.

. . . A CONFIDANT, BUT NOT A LOVER.

Hoping that you'll rescue me from future bad relationships, okay?

Not attracted to you in the least, but you do make me laugh.

"Don't worry about it, I got it"

THE LEAST YOU CAN DO IS OFFER.

I like playing the big shot.

I don't want you to have to worry about anything.

I'll pay again.

"Don't worry about it, I got it"

I told you several times, now I have to do it. Unbelievable!

STEP ASIDE, I'LL HANDLE THIS . . . GUTLESS WONDER.

You better get this if you know what is good for you.

Dude, it was a test and you failed. Don't worry about it now.

"I love your new hairstyle"

Wow, what a butcher job!

. . . WHEW! THAT WAS A CLOSE ONE. ALMOST DIDN'T NOTICE!

You have a new hairstyle?

You spent $150 on that and it doesn't even look different.

"You have to learn to communicate"

YOU NEED TO LISTEN.

I think we know each other well enough for you to open up to me and tell me what's going on.

If you know what is **good for you,** you'll agree with me.

If you don't open up, I'll just keep on talking.

"Have you lost weight?"

You've lost a ton of weight, but I can't say that, you'll think I'm insinuating you were fat before. Then I'll never get laid!

Maybe you should lay off the chocolate-covered, double-stuffed Oreos.

I'm trying to kiss your ass so that eventually you'll have sex with me.

You girls sure seem to like it so here goes, the obligatory question. . .

"SIZE DOESN'T COUNT"

Unless, of course, it's just too small.

Size totally counts, but you're cute and we can buy toys.

...Unless I can't have an orgasm.

IS IT IN YET?

"WERE TAKING A BREAK FROM EACH OTHER"

Let's see how long I can string you along.

My wife/girlfriend is in New York and I'm here on the West Coast.
There's no possibility of her finding out.

This is all a load of crap.
I just really want to sleep with you.

. . . She told me that if I leave her now, she'd take me for everything I've got.

"I need new shoes"

I'm depressed and need something to cheer me up.

YOU WANT SEXY?
I NEED NEW SHOES.

Get out your wallet.

FYI - I'M GOING SHOPPING. I will get new shoes AND a few other things "ON SALE."

"It would take too long to explain"

I HAVE NO IDEA HOW IT WORKS.

Believe me, you wouldn't care enough to hear the full explanation.

I don't understand it myself. It's too complex for me be able to fully articulate it. Any attempt would fall short.

By the time I explain it, I'll already have it fixed.

"We need . . ."

"WE" MEANING "US" AS IN "TEAM" AS IN HAPPILY EVER AFTER.

Posing the question as "WE" is a nice way of stating what I really want. Which is everything.

I need...

"I was wrong"

I could argue with you, but what's the point?
You always get the last word anyway.

THE THREE WORDS THAT ARE THE KEY TO ANY SUCCESSFUL MARRIAGE . . .

It's your fault **but I want make-up sex.**

I screwed up again. **Sorry.**

"I was wrong"

I'm never wrong

I'M NEGOTIATING. I'M A LITTLE WRONG, AND YOU'RE GROSSLY WRONG. NOW WE'RE GETTING SOMEWHERE.

I have a compulsive need to be right.
That's why this doesn't exactly sound sincere.

I was wrong, but not as wrong as you.

“You have beautiful eyes”

. . . THE REST OF YOU . . .
NOT SO HOT.

. . . Beautiful lips, beautiful hair, skin, nose, breasts. . .
Sleep with me. Now.

HERE GOES. OLDEST LINE IN THE BOOK.
WONDER IF SHE’LL BUY IT.

Oh, geez, let’s see.
What do I like most about you? Well . . .

“You have beautiful eyes”

I’m being hypnotized and I like it.

I’M GOING TO HAVE TO HIDE YOU
FROM ALL MY FRIENDS: YOU’RE HOT.

I see the “you” beyond your eyes.

STOP STARING AT ME.
You make me uncomfortable.

"Nice skirt"

Booty-licious.

. . . I'd love to get **underneath** it.

I've been checking out **your ass.**

You show off your **assets very well.**

"Are you willing to?"

This is not a question but a demand.

As long as I use the word "**willing**" you'll be more apt to do what I want. How's it working on you so far?

LISTEN, NOT TO SOUND KINKY, BUT WILL YOU. . .

You better do this, or else.

"NICE TOP"

YOUR BREASTS ARE
DRIVING ME CRAZY.

I'm taking notice. See, how I'm taking notice?
That should earn me some points.

. . . I can almost see your nipples.

Not enough material there
to call it a blouse, now is there?

"I feel safe with you"

It's good to know you'll always be here when
I go off and do something crazy with
those dangerous types.

I'M JUST NOT THAT INTO YOU.

I feel an important connection with you.
You are wonderful and cozy and
delicious all rolled into one!

Can I call you "Sugar Daddy?"

"SURE, GO AHEAD"

Anything to shut you up.

YOU'VE ALWAYS SUPPORTED ME.
SO NOW IT'S MY TURN. GO FOR IT.

I don't give a sh@*!

No skin off my nose.

"Sure, go ahead"

I dare you.

I WANT TO BE SUPPORTIVE,
SO I'LL ENCOURAGE YOU THIS TIME.

If you do this, don't expect me
to be here when you get back.

Go ahead. Sabotage yourself. SEE IF I CARE.

"I had other things on my mind"

I have no idea what you have been saying for the last 10 minutes.

. . . like getting laid tonight.

Can't a guy even have a thought?
Must you control everything?

. . . bills, bills, bills.

"I think we should slow down"

I need time to do a background check on you.

. . . PLANNING A WEDDING TAKES A LONG TIME.

I believe in foreplay! Got it? Slo-o-o-ow!

Okay, we just met.
Get your tongue out of my ear!

"Sure, I like kids"

AS LONG AS THE KIDS
DON'T BELONG TO ME.

I LIKE KIDS.
I don't always like what they do or say.

I have to if we're going to have sex.
I'm Catholic.

Not yet. **NOT YET.**

"Sure, I like kids"

I have to say I like kids or he'll think I'm an old-maid spinster and that my eggs dried up long ago.

KIDS GIVE ME CRAMPS.

I actually love kids. Adore them. Unless you don't. And then I can take them or leave them.
Mostly leave them.

I like other people's kids. **A lot.**

"I never cheat"

I've never been caught.

Do one-night stands count?

I'd have an affair,
if someone would make me an offer.

I've always RESPECTED the person I was with.

men women men women men women men women men women men women men women

"I never cheat"

I'm not a cheater. And remember that whenever you're tempted by some trashy cocktail waitress/airline hostess/co-worker. **I don't cheat.**
And if you do, I will make you pay.

I HAVE HAD AN AFFAIR BEFORE
BUT I LEARNED MY LESSON.

Cheat on me, and you'll find yourself
the star of an A&E true-life murder mystery.

I will know if you cheat, so don't even try it.

“We need to catch up and have a drink”

ARE YOU STILL INTERESTED IN ME?

....

We need to have sex
like we used to.

....

I was hoping I’d never run into you again.

....

I need to get you drunk enough to sleep with me.

“We need to catch up and have a drink”

Do I always have to be the man? I like you, I’m asking you out. You do the rest!

....

DUH, I’M INTERESTED.
ARE YOU?

....

Sure, I’ll hang with you
until I find a boyfriend.

....

As long as we keep it in the future,
I don’t have to deal with you now!

“I’m rethinking my career choices”

I’M THINKING ABOUT BREAKING INTO PROFESSIONAL SKATEBOARDING.

Your dad was right, “I’ll never amount to anything.”

I’ll **never** get anywhere in this dead-end job.

I GOT FIRED.

“I’m rethinking my career choices”

I have no idea what I’m doing with my life.

I LIKE BEING TAKEN CARE OF. WILL YOU TAKE CARE OF ME?

I’m quitting my job the day we get married.

Sugar Daddies’ are my favorite candy.

"I was working late at the office"

I WAS PORKING THE NEW SECRETARY.

Do I have to account for every minute of the day?

I was out GETTING DRUNK.

I'm tired of your nagging.

"I'm on my period"

Sex is definitely out of the question.

I'M CRANKY.
(MAKE ME FEEL BETTER . . . WAITING ON ME HAND AND FOOT MIGHT DO THE JOB.)

I don't want to be touched at the moment.

Do not show up here without chocolate, something salty, a funny movie and a really cool trinket.

"Your girlfriend is really nice"

HOW ABOUT A THREESOME?

. . . for a hater.

. . . Can I have her number?

. . . is she single?

"Your friend is really nice"

Finally, someone to fantasize about.

IF THIS DOESN'T WORK OUT, I'M CALLING YOUR FRIEND.

Your friend was hitting on me.

Exactly how close are you to your new friend? I'd like to sleep with him.

"Sure, I love foreplay . . .

Don't want to ruin my chances, so . . .

Arghh . . . you're torturing me!

Okay, but make it snappy.

Why waste time?
Let's get down to the nitty-gritty.

"Sure, I love foreplay . . ."

I love it when you tease me.

A-HA! HE'S TRAINABLE!

Sure, you go first.

This does not mean
turning the television off.

"Of course I'll respect you in the morning"

BUT CALL YOU AFTER WE HAVE SEX?
THAT'S ENTIRELY OUT OF THE QUESTION.

. . . **Why?** Are you a nymph or something?

. . . But might have some difficulty
with that right after I climax.

I'll say anything to get you
to take those clothes off.

"I'm not emotional or overreacting"

THANK YOU, Mr. Roboto. I'm NOT emotional,
I'M PASSIONATELY EXPRESSING myself.

I KNOW I'M OVERREACTING...
STOP POINTING IT OUT!

You did something wrong
and you need to acknowledge it.

Overreacting? OVERREACTING?
Baby, you ain't seen nothing yet.

"I'm ready for a commitment/relationship"

I need my green card.

. . . I think.

If this is an ultimatum, then yes. . .

Stop seeing that other guy.

"I'm ready for a commitment/relationship"

It's your face I want to see when I wake up. Your skin I want to touch when I make love. And your soul I want to feel. Now. . . and for the rest of my life.

I'M HAPPY THAT YOU HAVE COME AROUND AND ARE COMMITTED TO MAKING THIS RELATIONSHIP WORK.

THIS SUCKS. I need something that is more serious than our current situation.

I've picked out a giant diamond ring. wanna see?

"I'm NOT ready for a commitment/relationship"

I'M ENJOYING BEING A BACHELOR TOO MUCH.

We can sleep together but these are my terms.

Let's keep things light . . . I can't stand it when there are expectations.

I still want to SLEEP WITH YOU but don't want to have to MARRY YOU TO DO SO.

"I'm NOT ready for a commitment/relationship"

It's not a reflection on you "or my feelings for you. . .

I'LL LOSE MYSELF. THEN WHAT?

I'm enjoying being the object of others' affection.

Not wasting time with people that are not right for me. **This means you.**

"I feel like we're stuck in a routine"

What do you say you **let me tie you up?**

....

Why do you just lay there
when we're having sex?

....

Life sucks and you won't. **The end.**

....

I NEED MORE SEX.

"I feel like we're stuck in a routine"

We need to
spice up our sex life.

....

I WANT YOU TO BE MORE ROMANTIC AND SPONTANEOUS, AND SURPRISE ME MORE. I NEED YOU TO PAY MORE ATTENTION TO MY NEEDS.

....

I'm taking care of you all the time.
WHAT, AM I YOUR MOTHER?

....

EXCITE ME!!! Put a bit of effort into it!

"Do you get along well with your father?"

ARE YOU DADDY'S GIRL?

Why do you call me
"DADDY"
when we're making love?

What kind of issues
do you have with your family?

Do I need to **be afraid of him?**

"Do you get along well with your mother?"

Whose side will she
be on for arguments?

WHERE IS THE BAR SET WITH
GOOD OL' MOM?
DO I HAVE A FIGHTING CHANCE HERE?
WHAT DO YOU EXPECT FROM ME?

I'm trying to **psycho-analyze you** and find out
what **baggage you are bringing into
this relationship.**

Are you a mama's boy? How controlling is your
mother and how will it affect our relationship?

"I feel so close to you right now"

Er . . . um . . . can't think of anything romantic to say. HOW ABOUT THIS. . . ?

This is as vulnerable as I get.

This is a really small bed.

You're earring is caught on my chest hair.

"I feel so close to you right now"

Don't you hurt me
OR you'll pay for it later.

TELL ME YOU LOVE ME AND I'M YOURS.

How do you feel about the word
"FOREVER?"

I am starting to feel the "L" word, but I don't want to be the first to say it.

"I'm just so busy with work right now"

PLEASE TAKE THIS AS A NICE WAY OF SAYING "I'M NOT INTERESTED IN SEEING YOU ANYMORE."

You can count on my missing things like birthdays and anniversaries for a while.

I need some time to **make up** my mind about you.

YOU'RE TOO MUCH WORK, AND I ALREADY HAVE A JOB, THANKS.

"I'm just so busy with work right now"

Work is just work but I cannot stand another date where you ramble on about your comic book/ Japanese anime/porn collection.

I have five kids, sinking debt and an STD. I'm trying to do you a favor. **STOP CALLING ME!**

You have NOT IMPRESSED ME enough for me to rearrange my life for you. SORRY, BUDDY!

Comparatively…spreadsheets excite me.

YOU DO NOT EXCITE ME.

"We need to take a break"

An old girlfriend is
in town for the week.

I'm feeling trapped.

I'm a gutless wonder.

I'm trying to figure out
an easy way to let you down.

"We need to take a break"

I hate your personality but love
having sex with you.

SHOOT! I THOUGHT YOU
WERE GOOD MARRIAGE MATERIAL. NOW, WHAT?

. . . Doesn't mean you can sleep around though.

Yo, loser. Take a hint.
We are NOT getting back together.

"DO YOU LOVE ME?"

WHAT ARE YOU WILLING TO DO TO PROVE YOUR LOVE FOR ME?

I messed up big time and you're going to be really upset. But if I get you to say "I love you" maybe it won't be so bad.

I want to do something kinky.

My ego needs a rub!

"Do you love me?"

I'M SO IN LOVE WITH YOU,

I'm losing control. I need to hear you say it.

Just to make sure we're even.

CAN I BORROW MONEY? . . .

I SAW THIS NEW OUTFIT I'M DYING TO GET.

DOTE ON ME. Tell me I'm your absolute everything. Say you'd give your life for me. Then, we'll have sex.

I'm very insecure right now and need your attention. Tell me how much you love me and please say "yes."

"I like you but . . ."

I LIKE YOUR BUTT . . .
YOUR FACE LEAVES SOMETHING TO BE DESIRED.

You're nice.
I don't want to hurt your feelings.

I'm completely on the fence
about my feelings for you.

. . . I just don't see us being
together in the long run.

"I like you but . . ."

This is it, pal. End of the line.

. . . NOT ENOUGH TO SLEEP WITH YOU.

I haven't quite gotten
past the wart/mole/peg-leg.

I could see myself sleeping with you once
(if desperate), but beyond that . . .

“What’s wrong?”

What meaningless psycho drama
are you going through now?

I’m in deep shit, right?

Why are you acting so weird?

Which one is it?
. . . nothing, everything, or all the above?

“What’s wrong?”

DON’T MANIPULATE ME,
just tell me what you want.

STOP POUTING AND ACTING LIKE A CHILD
AND TELL ME WHAT’S WRONG SO
I CAN PRETEND TO FIX IT.

Not amused by the silent treatment,
but I’ll say the line anyway: WHAT’S WRONG?

Would you like some cheese
with that WHINE?

"I'm not angry"

I'M ABOUT TO SNAP. ANY MINUTE NOW.

. . . I'M FURIOUS.

I KNEW
I should have taken acting lessons.

God, you piss me off.
Of course I'm angry.

I'm pissed off and
you better figure out why.

Don't mind the *twitching*.
Of course *I'm not angry*.

YOU WILL PAY FOR THIS LATER.

I'm devising a way to get back at you.

"I'm not angry"

"I promise I'll pay you back"

HOPEFULLY YOU'LL FORGET ABOUT THIS "LOAN" BEFORE I HAVE TO PAY YOU BACK.

....

I'm really
grateful for your generosity.

....

I know, I'm a loser.
But I won't always be a loser.

....

. . . OR NOT.

"Whatever"

I totally disagree, but. . .

....

YOU'RE FULL OF
SH@*!

....

You're dismissed, moron!

....

SCREW YOU TOO!

"As soon as I finish this project, I'll . . .

(clean out the garage, take out the trash)"

Wait! Why does EVERYTHING have to be on your timetable?

I will put this off as long as possible or until you remind me.

Damn woman!
I can only do one thing at a time.

As soon as you agree to have sex with me.

"I don't want to talk about it."

...unless you don't want to know, it's best we drop the issue.

OH, I WANT TO TALK ABOUT IT. BUT FIRST I WANT TO GET MY THOUGHTS TOGETHER SO I CAN REALLY LET YOU HAVE IT.

I'm saving this as **ammunition** to be used against **you in the future.**

I'm a frenzy of emotions right now... back away from the conversation and get to safe ground.

"YOU'RE SO HONEST"

YOU'RE SO OPINIONATED.

I'm so DISHONEST.

You're self-righteous.

...TOO HONEST.

"You're so honest"

Thanks for being so TRUTHFUL. How about a little tact next time?

WHAT ARE YOU NOT TELLING ME?

Wow . . .okay . . . that was direct. I really don't need to know your every thought, actually.

I haven't caught you in a lie . . . yet.

"I am listening"

Why are you still talking?

Get to the **point** because
I don't have all day.

OOPS, BUSTED!

Just hurry up so I can talk!

It's killing me, but I really am.

"I am listening"

I'm **NOT** listening but **you don't usually notice.** Note to self - **fake it better.**

You'd better have one hell of a story.

Man, this guy likes to hear himself talk.
If I wanted that, I'd turn on Howard Stern.

. . . But you're not saying anything.

To Our Readers

Retired Hipster publishes books on topics ranging from personal growth to artistic expression to relationships. Our mission is to put out quality books that celebrate expression and nourish the human spirit– such as visual explosions in art, design and photography, as well as a full line of journals and gifts that will inspire you, make you laugh, and breathe new vitality into your life. We value integrity, compassion, and receptivity both in the books we publish and in the way we do business.

Our readers are our most important resource, and we value your suggestions, input, and ideas about what you would like to see published. Please feel free to contact us, to request our latest book catalog, or to be added to our mailing list.

Retired Hipster
PO Box 14068
San Francisco, CA 94114
www.retiredhipster.com